Beneath
the Gravel Weight
of Stars

Mimi German

A Publication of The Poetry Box®

Editing & Book Design by Shawn Aveningo Sanders
Cover Design by Shawn Aveningo Sanders
  using images licensed under Creative Commons

ISBN: 978-1-956285-00-0
Printed in the United States of America.
Wholesale distribution via Ingram.

Published by The Poetry Box®, March 2022
Portland, Oregon
https://ThePoetryBox.com

when the wood is too wet to burn
i will feed you melons   and the songs of birds

To all my brothers and sisters trying to survive on the streets in St Johns, Oregon, thank you for sharing your lives with me, your incredible courage, and your love. May you survive another night. I love you with all my heart. These poems are for you.

Contents

The Crossing

shadows cross the wired streets   the long dash of the horning
day   the slow roll of the sidewalk suitcase   the step of the
heavy cloud   deliberate the lift of the wet sneaker   the sod
of a prayer   she walks   hunting for cans   or love   to
feed the bear   last night's sun was turned off   the moon had
fled   today the forecast is too cold to be desperate   beneath
the unsnow of sky   one foot follows the other   regrettably
anywhere is the graveyard

The Other Side
of the Coffee Shop Window

his back sags against the crush of crescent moon   across the
shatter   beneath the gravel weight of stars   the fisted arms
of god   pleat to his back   shoving him forward   into the
sidewalk cracks   even the wheels of his cart are sullen   worn
bent from the handling and the crash of cosmic debris   the
bulldoze of shade across the seep   the concrete line   the
drunken dodge of burning snowballs   the head limp   the turn
aways   ursids whisper in the door jamb   over on 12th and
johnson   perseid hovels at the tracks   lyrids stoke a paper
fire   is it a star gown dance or the survival of lambs roasting
round the spit where wrinkles and jowls grow from no surprises
the rise   the fall   shallow waters   or high tide   his feet are
always wet

No. 19

earth on dry ink

waking tangled in the cling wrap morning sky
a sedentary rooster crows   a cold dog barks
squirrel hustles her nuts   busses croon on city
streets   the pothole begs   a tugboat fights a
chinese barge   crows dock on wires   winter's
emptiness flocks   cottonwoods expose the nest
worms earth themselves   the spate of day

No House Row

the oatmeal stain of six a.m. on the maggots grip of winter's fist   the dung heap canvas rustles on the hang of clothesline stench   grease the replay of a lost good day   head torque into bending lonesome   rusting spine of pleating shade covers the heavy curl of the unrecognizable suit and the hide of swollen fingers   this is no house row   where taut rinds sorrow and dreams decompose like weeds lamenting   where grasses die tucked in the nestle of sleeting rain   the limp dick honesty of a gray sky off-kilters your mask   hungry is the sag   the heart is yesterday's buttered squash and gristle tendered in the slow cook of hours

N. Fessenden

he wears the worn kilter and the right hand lean of the weight of
a man   torso bends heavy on his cane   waiting for a bus   he
turns a page in the cracks of the sidewalk   looks like burroughs
but i call him saint john   the necktie of hustle smears the greasy
air   potholes breed poets in these parts stammering like starlings
he is syntax framed   this is the garden   he is wild chard   city
workers paint the lines   kicked up stones crack the windshields
of the parishioners of the church of daylight savings where sun
seeps into cracks and the doors are always locked

Despite

the thorn of winter's buds   sprout the harp
strings of spring   beneath the wisps of the
bending branch   tent people murmur   huddle
round the candle fire   the sweet honey suckled
vine   it is 4 a m   dark tendrils retract
forsythia yawns   remnants of a leaf tuck into
mud   the pink tutu clings to the receding wing
of night   chimes of hellebores arch their backs
in the yawn   bluebird shuffles on the perch
the sheer ghost of morning

To Beggar

blueberries fall like dislodged stars   fingers paw the ground
searching scratching through the dirt   one tumbles   down
the ant hill   the chickens squawk at the laughing mole traveling
the bend of light down the slide in nine ripples which you know
when looking sideways is the angle of the sun   a hemisphere
of mirrored eyes   its edge indented tin   blue is the tiled dome
an ice ball clings to the rim of glass   clarity rides the cherry in
the dumpling of the donkey saddle   salmon eggs float on the
cracked backs of oysters   ribs of sunlight tall the trees clinging
to the nots that burn the feet   lavender begs to the sky between
the hours

Noon in the Park

he dragged in his hand   a three-legged chair   visible only to
him   it was made of oak or was it maple   the faded yellow
paint was chipping and one leg had fallen off   he found it this
way on the path   slowly like a tattered paper crane opening
he bent the tall sky beneath his thin body to sit on the invisible
chair   he wobbled for balance   crows spread out beside him
to hold on for the steady   the squirrels came by to see the
scene   the man on the invisible rickety chair stood up   pushed
the chair over   and yelled to all that all he wants is to have a
shower   he paused   and to clean his balls   he stood on one
foot   his other leg shaking like a crooked cane at the wind and
at the squirrels and at the sky   but then he bowed   a deep
quiet bow   humbling himself to the wet muddy ground   and
sat down once more   on his chair made of air

Afflicted

she holds her breath   as if she were holding god   when she
could no longer stand   when her eyes bulged like a blowfish
on a hook   she exhaled   and god let go of her   sometimes
she waited for angels to appear in the silence not knowing that
the silence was an angel appearing   the doctors said she was
afflicted   because she could not shut her eyes   she dreamed
she never slept   which wasn't a dream   she was the colors
of all things   and all things were she   in the early morning
hour   she would lie on the ground   feeling   the moon tied
tightly to her belly   she was its rock   tied to a tree   when
the ground swayed she laughed on her swing   as the moon
exhaled she tucked in the seasons' corners   she collected leaves
and sometimes dust   she walked the shimmering finless trail
of scales   the tiptoe of jangled light   she rubbed her skin
in luminescent sand to feel whole dipping her tilt into the lost
lake   uncertain of the footings   she knew the notes of wind
yesterday she met a young man who was high   on living   he
told her there is beauty   she thought he was a spirit   a truck
blew its horn startling her back into the stark   she inhaled

No. 36

gouache and pencil

her eyes of horse hair   a gulled oyster   she
is preemptively pretty   ancillary   but really
she is kali   he   her driver of mirrors who sews
into buttons a partial breath   his fingers inhale
the beauty of what isn't the day   cups her image
in his teeth   she is frost on the blink of a sun
in the back seat   the middle of eleven o'clock
inside her pants   his lips quiver   he mistakes
her for the milky way   or an arrow   full vision
fuckery   she tucks in to herself   then nods
into the dream

No. 7

ink on rag

stale   the hungry arc of morning   rooting
scruff   indian woman speaks to cellophane
trash stuck to the one-legged wheelchair   she
wakes a broken bird inside its bag   click clop
luminaries rush the crosswalks of the go right
ahead   of the yes by all means   the grunt
of welcome   phantoms blare the charcoal day
crows eat fallen scraps   the rot stink from last
night's swag

Streets of Gods

butchie felts a wide-brimmed hat   been scorching fire air for
weeks   the rope of fragile branches sway inside his faded jeans
he got a new red stripe shirt   i see him cross the lot   he bends
like a water bird   reaching   into the trash   one arm points
to god for balance   the other to the circus   he's looking good
handsome   angular   good-lookin' man   loosely bound   the
curve of his gray   a pony tail rides his spine   so castro today
a stub of a cigarette smokes curls around his worn bulbs   a
bronzed god   his thick nails carry earth   like hide   the street
tan   he is   poetry   where you been   he drawls   leans
into the car's half cracked window   hey i thought that was you
here and there   you know   been on the farm   yeah you look
good   where you been hangin   you know   at the cut   saw
they swept everyone the other day   yeah we moved to the other
side   you know   it's cool   what do you need   anything
yeah   yeah   nothin' really   i'm good   smoke comes out his
nostrils   his lips   he's on his horse   divine

Sides

the pea pods snigger from their towering poles as the weedy lot
through drunken privilege sleep   and soften   the boils and
shadows of the underground roil   the piggly-wigglies come
to snort and root in restless dreams   below the muzzle of
the barnyard grass deep inside the lambs quarters   we   the
underlay   are your goatshit   your hard earth   your targeted
pellet skeet   your mosquito bait   yours to burn in the thrush
of noonday swelter   your reason for your own shit lives   your
hundred tongues of spew and gobs of malice   you peckers of
inanity   you wilderness lost   you leathered hearts of forgotten
mothers   you roamers of the course salt   you who toss the
scrag   you who crack the black streets white   you the maggot
rose   we the hamstrung in the leafless drift   we the soldiers of
the scrum   we the desolate circumference

Northern Flats

crow teeters at the gutter with wings of a
drunken priest   minds his own damn business
in the sugar pan of the jaundiced sun   blue
jay flaps her squawk on a wind that isn't blowing
aims it high and direct   a straight shooter
crow dips and bows   spider spins the gargoyle
cloud   this beautiful day   cloud clings to sky
blue jay to crow   sky to the heavens   pollen
spreads its yellow   crow's night feathers glow
a golden air   blue jay bounces on the wobbly
branch   pulls back an arrow   crow ducks to
sip his drink

Unsheltered

we hide here   among the grasses and porcupine tellers of four-
storied lives   braided we thrush   then are shorn   or is it that
we live like shade   mullein leaves repel the sun   inside the
dandelion dome seeds rise to reach the mantled prayers   wind
cackles the bones of the dreaded spokes   unhoused wheels
spin on the low cycle   the bourbonous twilleries of the dirt
fairies dance   sticky pitch the starlight gaze   at us the mirror
cracks   at us   at us   where is reflection   the avenue of
sleepers hardens our shards   indigent rain on the relic road
we muddy drift deeper down the molaries mire   the same moon
in the town that shivs this windowless view   keeps a lover in
the lake for the fisher man's wife   on the lip of luscious insanity
we wither on this sog canal

Babel

beneath an orchard wing of pomegranate stars
the mountain grieves   leaves crumble in the
steps of wind   it's all overripe mangoes and dull
knives   cold vowels chatter   syllable hills tie
longhorn sheep to the pen   in the basement of
the order of things the word is stressed

No. 29

opaque pastel on crepe paper

her hustle   beneath headphones and a johnny
deuce   no rain   no wet   the bone shiv of
winter waits in the cracked lips of clouds   mean
time   thirteen cans is a free lunch   no dog is
doggin' today   lombard is the slot ma chine

When Are the Buds

i suffocate in this stench   curdled porridge congeals the rim
today's uncomfortable boots and the leftover wet pants moon
stink   like the miller's cheese cellar and the rotted mouse head
the torn of the opened tent   the ant zippered rind   skin of stale
cream in the coffee cup glare punctures goodness   argues against
the autumn rose   pungent licks the bannister's bitters   cruel
stench   the winds swing this foul   permeated clothesline of the
rotted holy sock   branches trapezed and fevered   scabbing
thick clot air in the roiling dumpster   dog shit stain on the tired
shoe   the church smudge chokes the corner lot   marshmallow
semen streaming the concrete dank   this cunnilingus air   the
daily bloat   sorrowed earth   when are the buds that hide the
thorns   my nostrils glue to the blanket stink   the bulge of bulb
nose statesmen   the parade of bloat   the pomegranate eyes
a bowery of stars in the mop slop bucket   fallen ash from the
chimney stack   skid the musty railroad ties   the wet stub
smoke   the lead sill lean   such an abundance   of chipped
beef stink   the breathe of breath   stale scour   drippings of
the slow cooked peasant   stench the cubicle square   rush
hour's daily   the swill of suit and tie   leggings run the ceiling
dinner burns the doll house down   the stank perfume warbles
the slough   monkeys toss their shit   old man gags on his spit
termites guard the cellar where the babies are buried   drool
tipped cigars smoke the board room priests   silent prayers from

row house row   a side dish of road kill for alms   when are the
buds that birth from thorns   nicotine sunrise combs the child's
pasty hair   the desert bloom heaves   cactus eyes the salve
souring on the vine   even a corpse scented death   has nothing
on this bloom   this 24 7 wilderness of stink   the vile loam of
night   its bacchus morning burp   and rancid dreams   the
lake drowns its fish   vase water turns the mustard gas   flower
heads loom   it's pruning time noon   the second hand circles
back   crow hops the mash of squirrel   pink worm curls into
melting flies when climbs the pearly hues of the pissed on picket
fence   to dive alive   into the empty pool   filled with fumes
and bitters

No. 13

river water and oil on cement

her face exposed   a crustacean shadow   hair of spindling
thorns   lips   splintered dusk   festering plums   back
straight   a schoolhouse chair   air dilates   swollen spores
burst   fish float past   belly up   the slow drift   the current
of chiseled weeds   seeds move like maggots on the stink of a
possum back   the yaw of prints in river mud

he folds the sun into creases   his legs   starved   eyes dart
then suspend   hummingbirds   umbrella fingers cradle threads
of sky   thigh to thigh   legs uncross   knee to knee   his shoes
are black   one lace is tied   the tide molts beneath his feet
his breath exhales exhaust   into the sullen wheeze

tilting   on the step   the swaggered limb   caught by the
concrete of a curried earth   skin color cholera   i know you
he said   can you bring me change   dry leaves turn to dust in
the moorings   tinsel ringlets melt on sidewalk   fingers bloat
in turbid water   do i know you   he squints into the sun

The Fallen

we are not perennial   not a flake of sap to flow

or root   our crump of aging torso falls   leaves

skate on hard fissured earth   frozen   the

wither   hagger   the cold varnish   the

leaf disintegrates into the crumble   truffled fir

boughs lick her curl   the raccoon shadow   the

broken twig of night   this icy pond

Trying to Find You

morning rise of sober sun   the cold hard   hourly misers walk
the slough   the chew of blue against the fold   over there
disgrace hangs gently on the curtain wing   a bird and then one
more root for bugs   a lonely hellebore prays to the ground   a
child dreams that all the rabbits lost their color and are falling
into holes   snow drifts the sad

now the sun a mile high   walks the lines of the house as if it
is still standing   where the roof once heaved now a sky crows
hawks watch from the smolder of air   speckled robins dissect a
worm   hydrangea heads frock in the almost of something   the
iris limp inside cracked earth and tomorrow called to say no

No.1

a metaphor in concrete

trampled hay feeds the straw of gnarled teeth   life is sparse
and glued to ground   this tilted painting of the donkeys
cracked   laughter brays like a knees-up drunk   water boils
on the cantankerous song of parrots   the rattle of chortle on
slop   there is a procession   of night crawlers   midnight rain
pounds the worms   thyme curls into winter's breath   oregano
remains the wild weed beneath the sleeping bag freeze   fiddle
ferns unfurl in praise of the briny sea and the sunset tongue   on
far away fields no god but a blanket   of wind   heart bones
hyperextend   un balanced on the bow

Day 50

she tucks her slink beneath the rickety socket
inside these bones of horns   birds   she crawls
into dreams past the man who stole the fallen
star for a twenty dollar bag

Dusty Canyon

tilting the sky on letters of wind   i cannot feel
he said   any more   not sadness   i have no
strands   his ponied hair out of synch across his
spiny river   dusty eyes of canyons mile   it's
all so very undone says crow shadowing the
rabbit hovering inside the moon dust swirls low
to ground   caw caw   peering rabbit bobs his
head   bicycle wheel rolls past he   pushed by
the dust of yesterday's ghosts

The Return

emerging   from beneath the cobblestones   he   corner of east
and west   crosses the downtown   between the chatter and
the avenue of geese   his voice a cockerel's crow   his flicker
the stub of a cigarette   its ash the city street   wingtips dare
the subway steam   the neon dart of unglued eyes   grate   a
specter in saffron   robes sandals and socks shuffles behind he
above a kernel of pigeons he   walks into the purpose   past
the doggerel of two dollar hand jobs   past   the one legged
whore   past   the melting ice of tree tops   the silver dreams
he inhales the alteration of earth's revolution   the hollow
aperture where the disfigured vine and the naked breast suckles
where fir dreams abort in marbled halls of the hallowed salad
he in the swagger of the setting sun   catches the swirl   before
the falling   leaf

He

the fray floats the ground like an unhoused child   a pregnant
robin parrots the sun braying like a mule   wheel barrows and
bicycles jump the fence   appearing through the nocturne he
wears a coat of falling feathers   walks the chapped sky   clover
tongues the fescue of the blue-eyed steep beneath his feet   he
curves toward the last left   past the open skirt of blossoms
where the crick of crickets hide   past the cring of spettels on
the long parade   then to the river of sunken oars   he   drags
the boat with the paper doll rudder to the shards of the twilight
banks   somewhere a broken violin slurs   he   has no wonder
of peacocks or prattle   a snail scuds gelatinous birth on the
crumple trail   wet lilacs glisten as if someone could remember
when   beneath the burdened hemlock   he   aligns the edge of
shore to hull then crosses over the bow foot first

Acknowledgments & Gratitude

Beneath the Gravel Weight of Stars (under the original title, *Eyes of Horse Hair*) was awarded honorable mention in The Hopper Poetry Prize (2020) and also a finalist in The Poetry Box Chapbook Prize (2021).

"Afflicted" appeared in *The Hopper* (2020).

"Hummingbirds" published in *Three Line Poetry* (#51, 2020).

∞

My deepest thanks to my partner, Jaylene, who loved me during and despite the countless hours that I sat beside the wood stove writing these poems.

Praise for
Beneath the Gravel Weight of Stars

"What does it mean to be housed in this increasingly complex world? What does it mean to be houseless? *Beneath the Gravel Weight of Stars* (formerly titled *Eyes of Horse Hair*) explores these questions with lyric, evocative constellations of images, where we see how lavender begs to the sky between the hours, and that shows—and evokes—so much, without having to be explicit. These brief poems reverberate beyond what is on the page, giving readers much to think on and feel long after the final page. Stunning music is scattered throughout all of these poems."

—Lisa Kwong, guest editor for The Hopper Poetry Prize

"These are very fine poems; I would not be ashamed to have written them! How I would like to see them in a book!"

—Cecile Pineda, author of *Entry Without Inspection*
and *Apology to a Whale: Words to Mend a World*

"These are beautiful and fierce and real."

—Steve Silberman, author of *Neurotribes*,
TA for Allen Ginsberg

About the Author

Mimi German is a poet, an activist, an organizer, and an advocate and co-founder of Jason Barns Landing, a houseless community and transitional village in St. Johns, Portland. She is also a co-founder of People's Housing Project based in Portland, Oregon.

Her poems have been published in *The Hopper*, *The Mantle*, *Three Line Poetry* (Vols. 51 & 52), *New Verse News*, and recorded and archived as testimony in Portland City Council sessions from 2017- 2020. Mimi divides her time between living in the remote wilderness of Steens Mountain and Portland, Oregon.

About The Poetry Box

The Poetry Box® is a boutique publishing company in Portland, Oregon, which provides a platform for both established and emerging poets to share their words with the world through beautiful printed books and chapbooks.

Feel free to visit the online bookstore (thePoetryBox.com), where you'll find more titles including:

Nothing More to Lose by Carolyn Martin

World Gone Zoom by David Belmont

Protection by Michelle Lerner

Gaslight Opera by Gary Percecepe

A Shape of Sky by Cathy Cain

A Long, Wide Stretch of Calm by Melanie Green

Moroccan Holiday by Lauren Tivey

Erasures of My Coming Out (Letter) by Mary Warren Foulk

Stronger Than the Current by Mark Thalman

Sophia & Mister Walter Whitman by Penelope Scambly Schott

What We Bring Home by Susan Coultrap-McQuin

The Kingdom of Birds by Joan Colby

and more . . .

9 781956 285000